<u>Top Tips for Survival</u>

<u>and</u>

<u>Success</u>

How anyone can be
successful and
"Live the Dream"

<u>Self-help and</u>
<u>Quick Reference guide</u>

Published by New Generation Publishing in 2022

First Edition

ISBN
Paperback	978-1-80369-550-1
Hardback	978-1-80369-551-8
eBook	978-1-80369-626-3

www.newgeneration-publishing.com

 New Generation Publishing

Testimonials

- "Top Tips for Survival and Success is a quick reference guide to survival and success in life. It covers most stages of life and offers readers helpful and insightful tips and is suitable for readers of all ages."

- "The book is laid out in a way that is easy to read."

- "The book has some of my favourite quotes listed as well as some very good guidance on many areas of life for everyone."

- "I can picture this book on a coffee table or in a manager's office."

- "The "About the Author" section at the end really tied the whole book together and did exactly what the book said it was going to do!"

- "…to give anyone looking for guidance a quick reference format, something easy to navigate and understand without having to bury their heads in large manuals and detailed study. (That they can do if they want to find more detail.)"

- "The author gives us the tools and reference to do just that and the goal of the book is clearly accomplished."

- "It has all the essential tips, quotes and pieces of knowledge to make a difference in all aspects of your life."

- "A handy guide full of helpful tips and tricks for life."

This book is dedicated to the person who, with her immortal words "If he/she can do it, so can you!", set me on my way! …my Mum.

Also, to the relatives, friends and business associates that have inspired and guided me along the way.

I've been very lucky to have known you all,

Thank You

Harj

Introduction

In an uncertain world where continual change now seems like the norm, everyone needs a little bit of guidance and reassurance.

As an enthusiast of self-development from a young age, over my life-time I've found and accumulated these useful tips. They have helped me through the hard times, …and offered me reassuring guidance through the good.

This quick reference guide has enabled me to find clarity, confidence and motivation if and when I have doubts,…and has guided me to achieve my desired lifestyle.

It has also been of assistance to friends and family of mine, so I'm making it available to you in the hope that you too will find it useful and helpful.

All of the tips can be related to life in general. (…and because I have an entrepreneurial passion, I've indicated those most relevant to entrepreneurs in blue font.)

Out of millions of tips, lots of advice and guidance out there, this is a selection of those that I have found most helpful and useful. Mostly from experts in their fields, some from famous people, others not so…but all that I've found inspirational and beneficial in some way.

(Those a little more relevant to our professional lives come first in the running order, followed by those with more relevance to our personal lives.)

The specific running order is given overleaf.

There should be something for everyone.

I hope that you will find these tips for survival and success helpful, as well as an enjoyable read and great to refer to whenever required.

Many Thanks and

Best of Luck!

Harj

foundr   •••

Warren Buffett
@itswarenbuffett

Surround yourself with people
that push you to do better. No
drama or negativity. Just higher
goals and higher motivation.
Good times and positive
energy. No jealousy or hate.
Simply bringing out the
absolute best in each other.

Contents

1. Steven Covey's 7 habits of highly successful people:...1

2. 20 Inspiring Quotes from Winston Churchill:.3

3. The Best Napoleon Hill quotes from "Think and Grow Rich" 6

4. Uplifting quotes from Great sportsmen and women 16

5. Tips from Successful Entrepreneurs............. 20

6. 10 self-care rules to live by if you work from home 22

7. From my personal wall of motivation (and a wide range of sources!): 25

8. How to Regain Your Positive Energy When Things Are Getting Tough 36

9. 12 Things To Do If You Wake Up Feeling Anxious 43

10. 13 Attributes of those considered Mentally Strong 49

11. Things Mentally Strong People Don't Do in Relationships 53

12. Gabriel García Márquez quotes.........................
.... 58

13. Keeping the relationship fresh ....
.... 62

14. How To Survive A Break-up (Because You Will).. 65

15. 10 Ways to Help Children Look After Their Mental Health... 66

16. The secret to enjoying a long life: 12 steps to help you be happy in later life......................... 67

Stephen R. Covey's book, The 7 Habits of Highly Effective People®, continues to be a best seller for the simple reason that it ignores trends and pop psychology, and focuses on timeless principles of fairness, integrity, honesty, and human dignity.

1. <u>Steven Covey's 7 habits of highly successful people:</u>

1. Be proactive.

2. Begin with the end in Mind. Define your goal, vision and mission.

3. Put first things first. Prioritise – do the most important things first.

4. Think win-win. Have an everyone-can-win attitude.

5. Seek first to understand then to be understood. Listen to people and understand their viewpoint.

6. Synergize. Work together to achieve more.

7. Sharpen the saw. Maintain, sustain and renew yourself. Taking plenty of exercise, rest, meditation, learning, training, etc, you will keep your body, mind, relationships and spirituality in balance.

Widely considered one of the 20th century's most significant figures, Winston Churchill remains popular in the UK and Western world, where he is seen as a victorious wartime leader who played an important role in defending Europe's liberal democracy against the spread of fascism. He is also praised as a liberal social reformer.

Churchill was Member of Parliament from 1900 to 1964, (except 1922-1924,) representing the Conservative Party and from 1904-1924, the Liberal Party.

2. <u>20 Inspiring Quotes from Winston Churchill:</u>

- "Attitude is a little thing that makes a Big difference."
- "Success is not final, failure is not fatal, it is the courage to continue that counts."
- "If you're going through hell, keep going."
- "History will be kind to me, for I intend to write it."

- "Never, never, never give up."
- "A pessimist sees the difficulty in every opportunity."
- An optimist sees the opportunity in every difficulty."
- "You have enemies? Good. It means you've stood up for something, sometime in your life."
- "I have never developed indigestion from eating my words."
- "When the eagles are silent, the parrots begin to jabber."
- "The price of greatness is responsibility."
- "Out of intense complexities, intense simplicities emerge."
- "I have nothing to offer but blood, toil, tears and sweat."
- "The empires of the future are the empires of the mind."
- "Courage is what it takes to stand up and speak, it's also what it takes to sit down and listen."
- "Continuous effort – not strength or intelligence – is the key to unlocking our potential."
- "Success is the ability to go from one failure to another with no loss of enthusiasm."
- "To improve is to change. To be perfect is to change often."

- "There is no time for ease and comfort. It is time to dare and endure."
- "Difficulties mastered are opportunities won."

Napoleon Hill was an American New Thought author. He is well known for his book "Think and Grow Rich" which has sold 20 million copies.

Hill's works insisted that fervid expectations are essential to improving one's life. May his quotes inspire you:

3. <u>The Best Napoleon Hill quotes from "Think and Grow Rich"</u>

1. "Both Poverty and Riches are the offspring of thought."

2. "Whatever the mind of man can conceive and believe, it can achieve."

3. "The starting point of all achievements is desire."

4. "No one ever is defeated until defeat has been accepted as a reality."

5. "Thoughts which are mixed with any of the feelings of emotions constitute a "magnetic" force which attracts other similar or related thoughts."

6. "Every adversity, every failure and every heartache carries with it the seed of an equivalent or a greater benefit."

7. "Poverty is attracted to the one whose mind is favourable to it, as money is attracted to him whose mind has been deliberately prepared to attract it, and through the same laws."

8. "All achievements, all earned riches, have their beginning in an idea."

9. "One of the most common causes of failure is the habit of quitting when one is overtaken by temporary defeat. Every person is guilty of this mistake at one time or another."

10. "One sound idea is all that one needs to achieve success."

11. "Success comes to those who become success conscious. Failure comes to those who indifferently allow themselves to become failure conscious."

12. "Wishing will not bring riches. But desiring riches with a state of mind that becomes an obsession, then planning definite ways and means to acquire riches, and backing those plans with persistence which does not recognize failure, will bring riches."

13. "There is a difference between wishing for a thing and being ready to receive it. No one is ready for a thing until he believes he can acquire it. The state of mind must be belief, not mere hope or wish. Open-mindedness is essential for belief. Closed minds do not inspire faith, courage, and belief."

14. "Remember, no more effort is required to aim high in life, to demand abundance and prosperity, than is required to accept misery and poverty."

15. "Faith is the starting point of all accumulation of riches."

16. "Faith is the only known antidote for failure."

17. "Ideas are the beginning points of all fortunes."

18. "Anybody can wish for riches, and most people do, but only a few know that a definite plan, plus a burning desire for wealth, are the only dependable means of accumulating wealth."

19. "The ladder of success is never crowded at the top."

More Napoleon Hill motivational quotes

- "There are no limitations to the mind except those we acknowledge, both poverty and riches are the offspring of thought."

- "Most great people have achieved their greatest success just one step beyond their greatest failure."

- "Any idea, plan, or purpose may be placed in the mind through repetition of thought."

- "Our minds become magnetized with the dominating thoughts we hold in our minds and these magnets attract to us the forces, the people, the circumstances of life which harmonize with the nature of our dominating thoughts."

- "When your desires are strong enough, you will appear to possess superhuman powers to achieve."

- "The starting point of all achievement is desire. Keep this constantly in mind. Weak desires bring weak results, just as a small fire makes a small amount of heat."

- "A goal is a dream with a deadline."

- "Opportunity often comes disguised in the form of misfortune or temporary defeat."

- "Whatever your mind can conceive and believe, it can achieve."

- "Every adversity, every failure, every heartbreak, carries with it the seed of an equal or greater benefit."

- "Great achievement is usually born of great sacrifice, and never the result of selfishness."

- "Everyone faces defeat. It may be a stepping-stone or a stumbling block, depending on the mental attitude with which it is faced."

- "If you do not conquer self, you will be conquered by self."

- "It is literally true that you can succeed best and quickest by helping others succeed."

- "Success is good at any age, but the sooner you find it, the longer you will enjoy it."

- "It takes half your life before you discover life is a do-it-yourself project."

- "Set your mind on a definite goal and observe how quickly the world stands aside to let you pass."

- "You have a brain and mind of your own. Use it, and reach your own decisions."

- "Victory is always possible for the person who refuses to stop fighting."

- "If you do not see great riches in your imagination, you will never see them in your bank balance."

- "When defeat comes, accept it as a signal that your plans are not sound, rebuild those plans, and set sail once more toward your coveted goal."

- "A positive mind finds a way it can be done; A negative mind looks for all the ways it can't be done."

- "Do it now!"

- "The way of success is the way of continuous pursuit of knowledge."

- "Don't wait. The time will never be just right. Start where you stand, and work whatever tools you may have at your command and better tools will be found as you go along."

- "Deliberately seek the company of people who influence you to think and act on building the life you desire."

- "You are the master of your destiny. You can influence, direct and control your own environment. You can make your life what you want it to be."

- "Strength and growth come only through continuous effort and struggle."

- "Most so-called failures are only temporary defeats."

- "Fears are nothing more than a state of mind."

- "Our only limitations are those we set up in our minds."

- "The cause of depression is traceable directly to the worldwide habit of trying to reap without sowing."

- "The more you give, the more comes back to you."

- "The man who does more than he is paid for will soon be paid for more than he does."

- "Think twice before you speak, because your words and influence will plant the seed of either success or failure in the mind of another."

- "Create a definite plan for carrying out your desire and begin at once, whether you are ready or not, to put this plan into action."

- "Some people dream of success, while others wake up and work hard at it."

- "You might well remember that nothing can bring you success but yourself."

- "The majority of men meet with failure of their lack of persistence in creating new plans to take the place of those which fail."

- "When you have talked yourself into what you want, right there is the place to stop talking and begin saying it with deeds."

- "If you give up before your goal is reached you're a quitter. A quitter never wins and a winner never quits."

- "Patience, persistence and perspiration make an unbeatable combination for success."

- "There is one quality which one must possess to win, and that is definiteness of purpose, the knowledge of what one wants, and a burning desire to possess it."

- "Plan your work and work your plan."

- "Tell me how you use your spare time, and how you spend your money, and I will tell you where and what you will be in ten years from now."

- "All the breaks you need in life wait within your imagination, imagination is the warship of your mind, capable of turning mind energy into accomplishment and wealth."

- "You can think your way into or out of almost any circumstance, good or bad."

- "Procrastination is the bad habit of putting off until the day after tomorrow what should have been done yesterday."

- "If you cannot do great things, do small things in a great way."

- "It is always your next move."

- "No one is ready for a thing until he believes he can acquire it."

- "Keep your mind fixed on what you want in life, not on what you don't want."

- "Hold a picture of yourself steadily enough in your mind's eye, and you will be drawn towards it."

- "Positive and negative emotions cannot occupy the mind at the same time."

- "Life reflects your own thoughts back to you."

- "Desire backed by faith knows no such word as impossible."

- "Action is the real measure of intelligence."

- "All thoughts which have been emotionalized (given feeling) and mixed with faith (expectancy), begin immediately to translate themselves into their physical equivalent."

- "You become what you think about."

- "You give before you get."

- "You can do it if you believe you can."

- "To be a star, you must shine your own light, follow your own path, and don't worry about darkness, for that is when the stars shine brightest."

4. <u>Uplifting quotes from Great sportsmen and women</u>

- "The more I practice, the luckier I get" Gary Player – Golfer, widely considered to be one of the greatest of all time.

- "If you fail to prepare, you're prepared to fail" Mark Spitz – Swimmer, nine-time Olympic Champion

- "Champions keep going until they get it right" Billie Jean King – Tennis player, winner of 39 major titles.

- "Hard work beats talent when talent fails to work hard." Kevin Durant – Basketball player, regarded as an all-time great.

- "In the end, it's extra effort that separates a winner from second place. It takes desire, determination, discipline and self-sacrifice. Put all these together, and even if you don't win how can you lose." Jesse Owens – Athlete who won 4 gold medals at the 1936 Berlin Olympics.

- "Sportsmanship for me is when a guy walks of the court and you really can't tell whether he has won or lost. He carries himself with pride either way." Jim Courier – Tennis player, former number 1 who won 4 "Major" and 5 "Masters" titles in his career.

- "A champion is someone who gets up when he can't" Jack Dempsey – Boxer, reigning World Heavyweight Champion from 1919 – 1926.

- "You miss 100% of the shots you don't take." Wayne Gretzky – Ice Hockey player, recognised as the greatest of all-time.

- "An athlete cannot run with money in his pockets. He must run with hope in his heart and dreams in his head." Emil Zatopek – Long distance runner best known for winning 3 gold medals in 1952 Olympics in Helsinki. In 2013, "Runners World" magazine selected him as the "Greatest Runner of All Time".

- "It's about you. If you win, it's you. If you lose, it's you. Black and white. Nowhere to hide." Greg Rusedski – Tennis player, former British number 1, US Open finalist and BBC Sports Personality of the Year 1997.

- "I've missed more than 9,000 shots in my career. I've lost almost 300 games. 26 times I've been trusted to take the game winning shot and missed. I've failed over and over and over again in my life…and that's why I succeed." Michael Jordan – Basketball player, claimed by some to be the best of all time.

- "Success is a process. During the journey sometimes there are stones thrown at you, and you convert them into milestones." Sachin Tendulkar – Cricketer, regarded as one of the greatest batsmen in the history of cricket.

- "When I go out there, I have no pity for my brother. I am out there to win." Joe Frazier – Heavyweight boxer, won Olympic Gold medal in 1964, and reigned as professional World Champion from 1970 – 1973.

- "I didn't aspire to be a good sport. "Champion" was enough for me." Fred Perry – Tennis player. Former world number 1 and the last British player to win the Men's Singles title at Wimbledon (3-times from 1934 – 1936) until Andy Murray in 2013.

- "Doctors and scientists said breaking the four-minute mile was impossible, that one would die in the attempt. Thus, when I got up from the track after collapsing on the finish line, I figured I was dead" Roger Bannister – Athlete, first to run a sub-4-minute mile (in 1954).

- "Some people believe football is a matter of life and death. I am very disappointed with that attitude. I can assure you it is much, much more important than that." Bill Shankly – Football Manager, best known for managing Liverpool to promotion to the First Division and going on to win 3 league titles and the UEFA Cup.

- "Every strike brings me closer to the next home run." Babe Ruth – Professional Baseball player regarded as one of the best of all time.

- "Age is no barrier. It's a limitation you put on your mind." Jackie Joyner-Kersee – Athlete, won 3 gold, 1 silver and 2 Bronze medals competing at four different Olympic Games. Voted Greatest Female Athlete of All-time by "Sports Illustrated for Women" magazine.

5. **Tips from Successful Entrepreneurs**

1. "Dream BIG. Start small. Most of all, start." – <u>Simon Sinek</u> (Leadership expert, Author, Motivational speaker)

2. "Your work is going to fill a large part of your life. The only way to be satisfied is to do great work, and the only way to do great work is to love what you do."– <u>Steve Jobs</u> (Entrepreneur, Co-Founder, Chairman, CEO of Apple Inc.)

3. "Surround yourself with people that challenge you, teach you, and push you to be your best self" – <u>Bill Gates</u> (Entrepreneur, Co-Founder of Microsoft, Philanthropist)

4. "Find a place that aligns with what you're trying to accomplish, and then just go for it" - <u>Tobias Lutke</u> (Entrepreneur, Founder and CEO of Shopify)

5. "One thing you can control is effort. Put in the time and effort to become an expert in whatever you're doing. It will give you an advantage because most people do not do this". - Mark Cuban (US billionaire entrepreneur)

6."Don't believe we have a "professional self" Monday – Friday and "real self" at the weekend. Just try to be yourself. Be honest about strengths and weaknesses, and encourage others to do the same" - Sheryl Sandberg (COO of Meta Platforms formerly known as Facebook)

7."Ask for help, you don't know it all. People love to help"

8. "Your worth is based on your ability to add value. But in order to do that, you've got to build the skills." – Tony Robbins (American author, coach, speaker and philanthropist)

9. "It's never a straight line to success, it's the bumps and divots that help you get there." Rick Goings (Entrepreneur, former CEO of Tupperware, founder of Dynamics Inc. and Federation of Youth Clubs.)

10."You cannot build a reputation on what you're going to do." – Henry Ford (Founder of Ford Motor Company, philanthropist)

> **Self-Care is a priority and necessity - not a luxury - in the work that we do.**

6. <u>10 self-care rules to live by if you work from home</u>

Self-care is vital when it comes to working from home. It's important to remember to create a distinction between your work and personal life, ensuring you take time out for yourself.

From taking a lunch break to making time to exercise and setting up a proper desk area, there are many ways to easily practice self care while productively working at home.

Business Insider have revealed the top self-care tips to remember when working from home.

1. **Set boundaries between your work and home** When you're not in the office, it's easy to slip into habits such as working late into the evening. In order to maintain a healthy balance between work and play, put clear boundaries in place so that there is a distinction between the hours you need to work and the time you have to yourself.

2. **Stock up on healthy treats**
   Keep your kitchen stocked up with tasty (and healthy) snacks to graze on during the day. A bowl of fresh fruit or nuts by your desk are a great way to keep hunger at bay in between meals.

3. **Try to fit in a work out**
   Making time for some light exercise will boost motivation levels and increase productivity. Even if it's a quick park run or 10-minute cardio workout in your front room, you will find yourself with more energy throughout the day. Walking or running with your dog is an excellent way for both of you to get in some additional exercise.

4. **Make time for a lunch break**
   If you regularly work from home, carve out time to give yourself a well-deserved break. Step away from your desk and head outside for fresh air.

5. **Create a meaningful morning routine**
   Whether it's heading out for a walk first thing or listening to relaxing music, get set for the new day by putting yourself first.

6. **Have a designated work space**
   If you have the space, create a small study area, with a desk and upright chair. Lighting is key to ensuring you don't strain your eyes, while a tidy area will help to keep your mind clear.

7.   **Take time to move during the day**
     If you work from home and don't leave your desk much, fitting in extra time for exercise is a great way to ensure you will keep fit and healthy.

8.   **Set a sleep schedule**
     Aim to get around eight hours sleep a night to ensure you have enough energy the following day. When you work from home, it can often be tempting to lie in later or stay up working.

9.   **Get dressed as if you're headed to the office**
     This will increase your productivity and get you in the right headspace.

10. **Meditation**
     Take some time to meditate during the working day and give yourself some headspace to completely unwind.

> No more Would've, Could've, Should've.
>
> The secret to getting ahead is getting started.

7. From my personal wall of motivation (and a wide range of sources!):

(Blue font indicates those most relevant to entrepreneurs.)

- 6P's for success:
    - Plan purposefully
    - Proceed positively
    - Pursue persistently

- Project yourself to age 80, and look back on your life.
    - You want to have as few regrets as possible.

- Just be thankful for what you've got,
    - ...don't take it for granted. Treasure it.

- Even under pressure
    - try to remain polite and positive.

- People have busy lives,
    - give them time, learn to be patient.

- It's nice to be important,
    - but it's more important to be nice.

- Treat everyone with kindness and respect.
    - Not because everyone is nice but because you are.

- Requirements for success:
    o Positive Mindset
    o Knowledge
    o Support

- Things I must not forget to say:
    o I'm so proud of you
    o I love you
    o You're Fantastic/Fabulous!

- Stress busters:
    o Meditation (Calm, Peaceful, Positive mind)
    o Sleep
    o Gratitude

...are closely connected with happiness and have also been found to reduce anxiety, envy and depression.

- We live in such an instant, entitled and comfortable society, ...that it can be easy to overlook what we have to be grateful for.
  - The best exercise for this is "Three Little Things". (Every night try to remember to write down three specific things you've been grateful for that day.
  - Read the lists frequently.

- Don't over-complicate

- The only impossible journey is the one you don't begin.

- No more Would've, Could've, Should've.

- Carpe Diem – seize the day

- Discipline is the bridge between goals and accomplishments (Source: Jim Rohn)

- Planning vs. Action – what is the optimum mix?
  - Need both for success.

- Specifically for entrepreneurs, need:
  - 1. Strategy
  - 2. Plan (to achieve the strategy)
  - 3. Sales
  - 4. Operations

- 5. Invoicing and chasing-up to get the money in.

- Cashflow is King.

- Mindset without Skillset will leave you upset, Skillset without Mindset will also leave you upset.
  You need both.

- Stay away from negative people, they have a problem for every solution.

- Where focus goes,
  Energy flows
  And Results show!

- Combatting potential burnout:
  - REST
    - R=Retreat
    - E=Eat Healthily
    - S=Sleep
    - T=Treat Yourself
  - Reset: Go for a walk to clear your mind
  - Exercise
  - Smile
  - Talk about the situation or write it down to get it off your chest

- You don't know what you've got until you lose it.

- Deal's not done until it's signed for on the dotted line.

- People will remember the way you make them feel.

- Two heads are better than one, (even when inexperienced).

  (Most relevant to entrepreneurs.)
  - Try to have a small nucleus of people who can help you.
    - (Maybe they have a different skillset which you don't have. For example, if you're great at Sales and Operations, and they are good at admin – that could be useful to stay on top of invoicing and getting the payments in.

  - Forecasting is crucial.
    - Try different scenarios
      - 1. You can change your cost price to more accurately reflect how much it actually costs you,
      - 2. Try different selling prices
      - 3. …and adjust your demand forecast to reflect sales levels at various different prices, depending on how competitive you are compared to competitor products.
      - 4. That will give you a forecast of your cashflow and profitability.

- Try to find a supportive person for encouragement.

29

- o Ideally, someone to turn to for advice
- o Someone to turn to for support
- o One that will also be honest with you to help improvement.

- No decision is "wrong", when made with what you knew at the time, in the position you were in and under the circumstances at that time.
  - o Then you should have no regrets.

- It's easy to take on too much. Always try to factor in the fact that you can only do one thing at a time.
  - o Learn to delegate
  - o Don't let enthusiasm or pressure make you take on more than you can manage
  - o It can lead to unhealthy stress and disappointment for both self and others.

- Celebrate success

- Sounds obvious, but it's an important point: Whilst planning is key, without actual sales, there will be no cash coming in.
  - o Get your product or service live as soon as possible, whether online, in a retail outlet or another route to market.
  - o Once listed you can change prices, etc.

- Please remember to eat well...
  It doesn't take long to prepare, for example, a hearty porridge breakfast, pasta, tuna mayonnaise.

- o Don't forget to eat when you're so busy you think you don't have time.
- o Food is your fuel, without fuel you will lose energy. You need energy to succeed!

- Driving long journeys can be a great time for clear thinking.
  - o Compared to the "noise" in the office when everyone plus the computer wants to give you information, - when in the car, you don't have these inputs…so can use the time to think of whatever you like.
    - o I suggest having a little list of what you want to think through (on your passenger seat). I have hands-free phone set up and when I come up with gems, (…or what I think are gems at the time!), I call my own number (i.e. the number of the phone I'm calling from!)…and leave myself a message (hands-free) that I can pick up later. Thereby, saving a potential gem of a thought which otherwise I might have forgotten.

- Just Do It… Impossible to predict everything that's going to happen, so just get on with it, because you will learn so much and that will help you to gradually optimise your offer.

- Whilst retail outlets and other routes to market, such as market stalls, are important in assessing customer reaction and feedback, online sales enable business to benefit from worldwide exposure and give you "Economies of Scale" which can multiply sales and profitability.

- Sales value minus Costs equals profit which is money to live on and to enjoy life.
  > Therefore, whilst profit margin is important,
- Sales are very important
- as is effectively managing costs.
  - o even 100% profit margin per sale is not great if you don't have a good level of sales.

- Once up and running, you need to find and employ a good accountant that will help you maximise profits by ensuring that all tax allowances, etc. are claimed where eligible.

- With regards to choosing an Accountant
  > bear in mind they're in business to make money,
  > therefore, they charge you for every little thing they do
  > so, in order to keep these costs down, I developed trackers that enable me to do most of the "book-keeping" myself, which is basically keeping records of income and costs.
  > For example, I logged and kept every receipt, in a plastic sleeve, one for each month, and preferably in order so that it takes one hour per month to actually add them onto a spreadsheet. (Two people doing that together takes 30 minutes per month.)

- Keep on top of the numbers.
  - Benefits of this are, firstly you can see if you're in profit (such as the daily tracker spreadsheet you should be doing)
  - Secondly, it will save you a lot of money, - remember even if the accountant only charges you £10 a day for your book-keeping, that would be £50 a week, ...which over a year is £2600. This is money straight out of your profit. ...
    - I think that would be a nice tidy sum to help pay for something such as a well-deserved holiday!

- If you're able to keep on top of your numbers
  - Then you can basically give your tracker, receipts and bank statements to the accountant
  - So they can do the actual accounting and advise on tax mitigation, - which is actually their area of expertise and what they should be doing (rather than being an expensive book-keeper doing your daily admin).

- Set Targets
  - Specific, Measurable, Achievable, Realistic, with Time-scales. ("SMART")
  - Don't worry about not hitting your targets every single week
  - … it gives you the opportunity to work out how to achieve them going forward.
    - There can be many reasons for fluctuations.
    - You want to find out the reasons for any fluctuations.

> As long as your financial position allows, you can achieve the targets within an agreed/planned timescale.
> Ideally, targets should not create unreasonable pressure ... the key thing is learning where there is room for improvement and opportunity to progress.

- Keep every receipt. If the taxman ever wants to know where you spent your money, it is very helpful to just dig out the receipts.

- You can pay somebody up to £100 a week cash in hand (as long as you keep records of it) and it does not affect any benefits they might be receiving.

- **For Entrepreneurs: Questions for the Accountant**
  1. How can I pay myself tax efficiently?
  2. How can I pay my employees most efficiently?
  3. How much will you charge to run the payroll process?
  4. What is the process for giving you daily sales and cost information?
  5. What would be the best company structure? Sole trader, Partnership, Limited Liability Company or Limited Liability Partnership.
     > Reasons why?
  6. Any other business.

- Try and develop additional income flows - gives you a buffer if one fails.

- Generally, in business there will be an 80:20 scenario. 80% of sales or profit will come from 20% of your customers. It is vital to know who is in the 20% and look after them because they account for the majority of sales or profit, maybe both!

- It can be lonely at the top. …try to develop outside interests.

8. <u>How to Regain Your Positive Energy When Things Are Getting Tough</u>

- Positive thinking is a mental and emotional state of mind that focuses on the good and expects positive outcomes. Developing and maintaining a positive attitude involves more than merely thinking happy thoughts. It is the anticipation of good (i.e. happiness, health and success) and it is the belief that all things–situations, obstacles and difficulties–will work out favorably in the end.

Optimism does not involve ignoring negativity. It is the acknowledgement of the negative but then choosing to focus on the positive. At its root, it is simply the belief that despite the current circumstance's things will work out favorably in the end. A positive mind comes from a heart full of faith.

20 ways to revive positive energy

Staying positive can be tough. Optimism stares obstacles in the eye and consciously chooses to look past them and believe… The problem comes in when the obstacles begin to obstruct optimism's view. Positivity can start to wane when you are bombarded with a succession of negativity, failures, disappointment and heartbreak. Every challenge we face withdraws from us energy, resilience and a little bit of our faith. Once your positive resources (energy, resilience and faith) are depleted, pessimism slowly begins to creep in and take hold. Below is a list of 20 things you can do to help revive your positive energy:

1. Enjoy nature

Research shows that reveling in the great outdoors promotes human health. Spending time in serene natural environments has been scientifically proven to lower stress levels, improve working memory and provide a sense of rejuvenation.

2. Perform random acts of kindness

Finding ways to put a smile on the face of others affects you just as much as it affects them. It takes the focus off of you and your problems and allows you to be a positive force in the lives of others. Doing good for others makes you feel good. It lifts your mood, improves self-esteem and self-worth and it serves as a small distraction from your current challenges.

3. Develop an attitude of gratitude

Noticing and appreciating the positives in our lives is a great way to lift your spirits and provide yourself a mental boost.

4. Take a mental break

Exhaustion is the silent killer of positivity. Learn to take breaks when things get overwhelming. Do something that gives your mind a break from whatever challenge you are facing–and that could just mean taking a nap.

5. Laugh

Laughter truly is the best medicine for most of what ails us. Laughter strengthens your immune system, boosts mood, diminishes pain, and protects you from the damaging effects of stress. Find a way to laugh–often. Watch a comedy, spend the evening with your crazy friend who knows how to keep you in stitches. Host a game night with your friends. Find a way to laugh.

6. Hang around positive people

Research suggests that stress is contagious — and the more you surround yourself with it, the more likely you are to let it affect your thoughts. In the same way that stress and negativity are contagious, so is happiness. The bottom line here is our behavior and thought patterns mirror those we hang around. Choose carefully who you allow into your circle.

7. Look for the silver lining immediately

Trying to force optimistic thinking amidst emotional turmoil or a bit of a shock usually doesn't work that well. However, training yourself to look for the lesson and find the bright spot not only eases the burden a little it will also slowly begin to transform your entire thought process

8. Breathe deeply

Breathing exercises help expel toxic air from your body and refill your body and, more importantly, your brain with fresh air. It clears your mind and allows you to regain mental clarity. One moment of clarity at the right time can change everything.

9. Don't dwell on negativity

Avoid dwelling on downers… downers bring you down! Focusing on negatives isn't just unpleasant, it also can make you less effective in tackling other tasks you face. Negativity produces more negativity. Bad things happen–try not to replay them over and over and fixate on unpleasantries.

10. Engage in positive self-talk

Talk to yourself. Tell yourself things are going to turn around and will work out in the end. Say it out loud. Speaking what you believe out loud reinforces and strengthens the message. You say it and hear it simultaneously.

11. Talk it out with a friend

Find a positive friend (or small group of friends) or confidant to talk to. Talking helps you hear the problem, admit and discuss your feelings and it gives you another set of eyes and ears working on the problem. You may find that brainstorming with another person or even a group will help you come up with new ideas to help you resolve the issue. It also reassures you that someone has your back and that emotional support makes a difference. Think of it as low-budget therapy.

12. Take a walk

Scientists have found that one of the best ways to chase the blues away is by going for a walk. A brisk walk calms you down by sparking nerve cells in the brain that relax the senses.

13. Engage in rigorous exercise

Getting sweaty is not just good for your heart–it's good for your head too! Research on anxiety, depression and exercise shows that the psychological and physical benefits of exercise help reduce anxiety and elevate your mood. When you engage in vigorous physical activity, "feel good" brain chemicals (neurotransmitters, endorphins and endocannabinoids) are released that ease feelings of negativity, distract you from your issues, and physically relax you.

14. Sleep

Proper rest is a critical part of maintaining a positive attitude. Studies have shown that even partial sleep deprivation has a significant effect on your mental state. Researchers from University of Pennsylvania discovered that subjects who were limited to less than 5 hours of sleep a night for one week felt significantly more stressed, angry, sad, and mentally exhausted.

It's hard to maintain a positive mindset under those conditions. Get some sleep!

15. Journal

Journaling is a great way to deal with overwhelming emotions. It provides a healthy outlet in which you can express yourself, manage your emotions and overall mental health. Keeping a journal can help you identify and track the causes of negative thinking and develop a mitigation plan.

16. Play Hooky

Taking the occasional break from the daily grind is fun, freeing and necessary. Figure out what makes you feel alive and happy and do that. Whether it's watching Netflix in your pajamas all day or if it's kayaking down a river – the goal is to have fun – whatever that means to you.

17. Treat Yourself

Rewarding yourself with "me time" and celebrating who you are as a person is vital to sustaining a positive outlook. Find small, meaningful and healthy ways to indulge yourself from time to time.

18. Move through your day mindfully (be fully present in every moment)

Worrying and dwelling on pervasively stressful thoughts are optimism assassins. Living mindfully involves conscientiously deciding to be fully present in each moment. When you throw all of your attention, energy and resources on the now you don't have the space for negative thoughts or worrying.

19. Take care of yourself spiritually

Paying attention to and investing in yourself spiritually is something most people neglect. You watch what you eat, workout, try to get enough sleep and do all the things you should to keep your body and mind fit and functioning. But part of maintaining good mental health and a positive state of mind is soul care. Take time to feed your soul and keep the mind- body-spirit connection strong by engaging in spirit enhancing, contemplative activities such as meditation, prayer, reading spiritual materials and/or attending religious services.

20. Celebrate small wins

Who doesn't love a good celebration? Celebrating small victories is one of the quickest ways to give negativity the boot. Getting out of bed this morning is a win! Celebrate it. If you stayed in bed today and got a little extra rest–that too is a win! Instead of focusing on pending doom or sulking over losses–actively seek out and celebrate the things you do well and the things you did get right today.

9. <u>12 Things To Do If You Wake Up Feeling Anxious</u>

For some, finding happiness is an everyday battle. Britain is facing a mental health epidemic as services fail those who need them the most and more people than ever are falling into crisis.

Anxiety isn't picky. It can creep in at any time of the day — even first thing in the morning. And before you know it, you're fretting about the future when your present day hasn't even started yet.

"Although there can be an almost infinite number of reasons why some people wake up anxious, at some point the mind starts traveling out into the future, whether that's a few minutes into the future or decades," Mark W. Driscoll, licensed clinical psychologist at The Family Institute at Northwestern University, told HuffPost. "Although that can seem productive — like we're just trying to work something out or solve a problem — it has the consequences of feeding and amplifying an already difficult-to-experience emotion."

Luckily, there are several techniques you can practice to help you better deal with whatever it is that's causing you worry. Below are some research and expert-backed tips to try if you wake up feeling anxious:

Before Bed
Put your devices on silent and keep them out of sight.
Late-night news notifications, celeb tweets or a conversation in a group text can all wait till morning. All of these alerts keep your brain buzzing, and make it harder for it to reach a state of relaxation. Plus, the blue light from screens can disrupt your sleep, and it can also prevent your body from producing melatonin, a hormone that's key for a regulated sleep cycle. It's well-established that poor sleep quality is closely linked with feelings of anxiety. You deserve a rest, as do your devices.

Set out your clothes for tomorrow.
Your closet might be packed with items you love — but all of those options can lead to decision fatigue, or the exhaustion and stress that's associated with having too many options to choose from. Getting dressed in the morning sounds like a simple task for any adult, but for some, it really can be wearing. If this sounds like you, try setting out your outfit the night before to see if doing so can help combat some of that morning stress. This process is you looking out for your future self, alleviating some of the jitters that come after sunrise.

Allot yourself some chill time.

Rather than jumping into bed for shuteye seconds after you finish up a work email, give yourself some relaxation time free of to-dos (and phones). Your body and brain will benefit from a wind-down period, which would ideally be an hour before your bedtime, according to the National Sleep Foundation. Relaxation reduces cortisol, the stress hormone that can increase your blood pressure and heart rate. Relaxation techniques like meditation, gentle movements like yoga and simple exercises like deep breathing can all help cut out the cortisol and promote better sleep. Whatever works for you to take some chill time for yourself, do it.

Try some mental exercises.

Instead of focusing on all you have to tackle the next morning, practice some mindful exercises. You can even turn it into a game: Try to recall as many dog breeds as possible, or mentally walk yourself through every room of your childhood home. This practice can help you keep anxious thoughts away while getting you one step closer to dreamland.

Reflect on the positive aspects of your day.

Especially if you're a worrier, training your brain to think about positive events instead of dwelling on negative ones can help you feel less anxious. The action distracts your brain from spiraling down a dark hole, and can make you feel more optimistic. If negative thoughts creep in while you're trying this, don't panic: Let them pass through and return to sunnier thinking.

"The idea is to get out of your mind and into your present-moment experience with soothing activities and to keep bringing your mind back to the activities when it wanders to worry thoughts or thoughts about the future," Driscoll said, adding that journaling about your worries before bed isn't a great idea. "A lot of people mistakenly believe that it helps and it usually has the effect of reinforcing and strengthening worries."

Hit play on a relaxing song.
"Blissful Mind" voted best and most relaxing song ever made on You Tube — can help you enter a state of relaxation. In a study of the song's effect, some people even reported feeling sleepy after listening. But if that doesn't work, put on a tune that personally soothes you.

In the morning, let your phone be.
Do yourself a favour and resist the urge to see if an overseas client responded to your email. Just as your devices can stress you out before bed, they can frazzle your brain first thing in the morning. Instead of waking up to a list of things you've missed or need to tackle, allow yourself to just be in the present moment of your morning.

Reframe your anxiety by acknowledging it.
"Noticing that you're anxious, responding to it in a way that says, 'It's bad. I hate this emotion. What if it never goes away? I have to get rid of it,' has the effect of intensifying the emotion and keeping it around," Driscoll said.

When you do this, anxiety becomes something else to be anxious about. "A way to let go of the struggle is to build skills in service of acceptance and acknowledgment of the emotion," he added. "Remember that acceptance is not the same thing as approval of or liking anxiety. Practice acknowledging anxiety by saying, 'Yes, I am feeling anxious right now.'"

Schedule some time just for yourself.
Ditching your morning phone habit may give you the extra time you need to start your day off right, but if you really want to soak up your free time, consider setting your alarm a little bit earlier. Having some time for yourself to engage in activities that can benefit your brain — like reading the paper or meditating — can set the tone for the rest of your day. Those extra minutes are beneficial even if they just allow you to feel less rushed as you prepare yourself for the day.

Breathe.
You don't even have to get out of bed for this one. Breathing is a power tool in reducing anxiety because it calls upon your body's relaxation response. Try inhaling to the slow count of four, noticing as your belly, ribcage and chest fill with air, then slowly exhale for the same count. You can use this trick at any time of day to find some relief.

Move your body.
You don't have to go to a workout class to reap the anxiety-relieving benefits of exercise (though, if you enjoy a sweat session first thing in the morning, by all means, keep it up). Maybe you can squeeze in a walk

around your block, or perhaps you can practice some yoga in your living room with the help of a favorite app or video. Just getting some physical movement into your morning can help you feel more calm.

Remember that anxiety is a normal human emotion to feel.
Bottom line: Don't shame yourself for how you feel. Driscoll said anxiety exists for a reason, and you don't need to brush it off as a problem that's "all in your head."

"There are legitimate problems in people's lives setting off anxiety," he said, adding that behavioral therapy practices and mindfulness-based stress reduction "have some of the strongest evidence bases out there for helping people let go of the struggle with anxiety."

So while this list provides a bunch of useful techniques that can work for one person, another may need more professional support to start feeling relief and that's OK.

10. <u>13 Attributes of those considered Mentally Strong</u>

Mentally strong people have healthy habits. They manage their emotions, thoughts, and behaviors in ways that set them up for success in life. Check out these things that mentally strong people don't do so that you too can become more mentally strong.

1. They Don't Waste Time Feeling Sorry for Themselves

Mentally strong people don't sit around feeling sorry about their circumstances or how others have treated them. Instead, they take responsibility for their role in life and understand that life isn't always easy or fair.

2. They Don't Give Away Their Power

They don't allow others to control them, and they don't give someone else power over them. They don't say things like, "My boss makes me feel bad," because they understand that they are in control over their own emotions and they have a choice in how they respond.

3. They Don't Shy Away from Change
Mentally strong people don't try to avoid change. Instead, they welcome positive change and are willing to be flexible. They understand that change is inevitable and believe in their abilities to adapt.

4. They Don't Waste Energy on Things They Can't Control

You won't hear a mentally strong person complaining over lost luggage or traffic jams. Instead, they focus on what they can control in their lives. They recognize that sometimes, the only thing they can control is their attitude.

5. They Don't Worry About Pleasing Everyone

Mentally strong people recognize that they don't need to please everyone all the time. They're not afraid to say no or speak up when necessary. They strive to be kind and fair, but can handle other people being upset if they don't make them happy.

6. They Don't Fear Taking Calculated Risks

They don't take reckless or foolish risks, but don't mind taking calculated risks. Mentally strong people spend time weighing the risks and benefits before making a big decision, and they're fully informed of the potential downsides before they take action.

7. They Don't Dwell on the Past

Mentally strong people don't waste time dwelling on the past and wishing things could be different. They acknowledge their past and can say what they've learned from it. However, they don't constantly relive bad experiences or fantasize about the glory days. Instead, they live for the present and plan for the future.

8. They Don't Make the Same Mistakes Over and Over

Mentally strong people accept responsibility for their behavior and learn from their past mistakes. As a result, they don't keep repeating those mistakes over and over. Instead, they move on and make better decisions in the future.

9. They Don't Resent Other People's Success

Mentally strong people can appreciate and celebrate other people's success in life. They don't grow jealous or feel cheated when others surpass them. Instead, they recognize that success comes with hard work, and they are willing to work hard for their own chance at success.

10. They Don't Give Up After the First Failure

Mentally strong people don't view failure as a reason to give up. Instead, they use failure as an opportunity to grow and improve. They are willing to keep trying until they get it right.

11. They Don't Fear Alone Time

Mentally strong people can tolerate being alone and they don't fear silence. They aren't afraid to be alone with their thoughts and they can use downtime to be productive. They enjoy their own company and aren't dependent on others for companionship and entertainment all the time but instead can **be happy alone**.

12. They Don't Feel the World Owes Them Anything

Mentally strong people don't feel entitled to things in life. They weren't born with a mentality that others would take care of them or that the world must give them something. Instead, they look for opportunities based on their own merits.

13. They Don't Expect Immediate Results

Whether they are working on improving their health or getting a new business off the ground, mentally strong people don't expect immediate results. Instead, they apply their skills and time to the best of their ability and understand that real change takes time.

11. <u>Things Mentally Strong People Don't Do in Relationships</u>

Most of us remember a crazy relationship we were in, or a time we acted crazy toward someone we love. Looking back, it's often difficult to remember what our mindset was at that moment. We ask ourselves, "Did I *really* act like that?" I wish I knew then what I know now about how to be a better partner, son/ daughter and friend.

The sad reality is that we just aren't taught how to be mentally strong when faced with adversity. The good news is that it's never too late to start. Here are 10 things mentally strong people DON'T do when it comes to relationships.

1. They don't analyze everything

Mentally strong people don't analyze the meaning behind everything someone else does. As an introvert, I pride myself on my ability to find the deeper meaning in life. But I caution you not to get too caught up in analyzing everything! Sometimes a head scratch is just a head scratch. (It doesn't mean they are bored with you and would rather be with someone else.)

2. They don't believe the other person will "complete" them

Mentally strong people complete themselves before they look for someone else to enhance their lives. You have to enjoy your own company first and nobody else can replace that part of you. Many people live their lives as if they were a character in a romantic comedy, and believe that they must eat, sleep, and breathe for their partner. Mentally strong people remind themselves they are complete just the way they are.

3. They don't bring up the past to justify the present

Mentally strong people don't bring up the past to win an argument or use it as relationship collateral. They try to work toward improving the relationship in that moment, instead of bringing up past events to justify their actions. Mentally strong people seek to live in the moment by understanding that the past has its place but will never solve today's problems.

4. They don't look outside the relationship to improve the relationship

Mentally strong people devote their full attention to themselves and their partner, when it comes to fixing problems in the relationship. They don't seek another person to fulfill their needs. They don't become distant and justify their behavior by looking outside of the relationship to feel better about themselves. They don't engage in destructive behavior to avoid the inevitable.

5. They don't put the other person down to feel better about themselves

Mentally strong people understand that you don't treat other people this way. It's a lot easier to blame someone else for the way you act or feel, instead of looking at *why you react* the way you do. Mentally strong people know that the only way to have a successful relationship is to lift the other person up, not put them down in order to temporarily feel better about themselves.

6. They don't stop communicating

Mentally strong people communicate with others in the good times and in the bad. They don't avoid conversations that need to be had. They seek to better understand their partner, instead of avoiding topics that are uncomfortable or awkward. The mentally strong don't avoid things because they are uncomfortable, but rather look at these situations as welcome opportunities to improve the relationship.

7. They don't stop loving themselves

Mentally strong people love themselves first, so they can love other people, *not* the other way around. Mentally strong people spend time improving their lives first, before they try and help anyone else. They know that by radiating love, it will only help the relationship succeed. Mentally strong people put themselves first.

8. They don't believe they can fix the other person

Mentally strong people help their partners in any way they can, but they understand that they cannot change the other person. Only an individual can change themself. Mentally strong people don't live in the future and convince themselves that if only they put enough effort or time into someone, then that person will change. Moreover, mentally strong people seek to understand the other person's perspective, before they try to offer them advice.

9. They don't try to make relationships progress faster

Mentally strong people accept that the relationship will develop in the right way. Of course, there are ways to improve the relationship and develop a deeper understanding of one another. However, mentally strong people know deep down that they can't force something that will take time to develop. They give up control and surrender to the natural progression of the relationship.

10. They don't stay in unhealthy relationships

Mentally strong people know when a relationship of any kind is no longer working. Not only do they look out for themselves, but they look out for the other person by communicating clearly. They understand that they've put in as much time and effort as they could, but would rather spend that time on someone who is right for them. The mentally strong know that everything will work out just fine.

It's a lot easier to find fault in someone else, especially when we become vulnerable and trust someone we love. I encourage you to be mentally strong first, then to seek someone who complements who you already are. Only through self-discovery can we better understand the types of people who will enhance our lives.

To successfully improve any relationship, you no longer seek to change the other person, but you will instead seek to continually enhance a long and prosperous life together.

12. <u>Gabriel García Márquez quotes</u>

"What matters in life is not what happens to you but what you remember and how you remember it."
— **Gabriel Garcia Marquez**

"It is not true that people stop pursuing dreams because they grow old, they grow old because they stop pursuing dreams."
— **Gabriel García Márquez**

"No medicine cures what happiness cannot."
— **Gabriel García Márquez**

"Nobody deserves your tears, but whoever deserves them will not make you cry."
— **Gabriel García Márquez**

"It's enough for me to be sure that you and I exist at this moment."
— **Gabriel García Márquez, One Hundred Years of Solitude**

"There is always something left to love."
— **Gabriel García Márquez, One Hundred Years of Solitude**

"He was still too young to know that the heart's memory eliminates the bad and magnifies the good, and that thanks to this artifice we manage to endure the burden of the past."
— **Gabriel García Márquez, Love in the Time of Cholera**

"She would defend herself, saying that love, no matter what else it might be, was a natural talent. She would say: You are either born knowing how, or you never know."
— **Gabriel García Márquez, Love in the Time of Cholera**

"nothing in this world was more difficult than love."
— **Gabriel García Márquez**

"All human beings have three lives: public, private, and secret."
— **Gabriel García Márquez, Gabriel García Márquez: a Life**

"Human beings are not born once and for all on the day their mothers give birth to them, but ... life obliges them over and over again to give birth to themselves."
— **Gabriel García Márquez**

"wisdom comes to us when it can no longer do any good."
— **Gabriel García Márquez, Love in the Time of Cholera**

"A true friend is the one who holds your hand and touches your heart"
— **Gabriel Garcia Marquez**

"...time was not passing...it was turning in a circle..."
— **Gabriel García Márquez, One Hundred Years of Solitude**

More Gabriel García Márquez quotes:

"I love you not for whom you are, but who I am when I'm by your side."

"Just because someone doesn't love you as you wish, it doesn't mean you're not loved with all his/her being."

"The worst way to miss someone is to be seated by him/her and know you'll never have him/her."

"Never stop smiling not even when you're sad, someone might fall in love with your smile."

"You may only be a person in this world, but for someone you're the world."

"Don't spend time with someone who doesn't care about spending it with you."

"Maybe God wants you to meet many wrong people, before you meet the right one, so when it happens you'll be thankful."

"Don't cry because it came to an end, smile because it happened."

"There will always be people who'll hurt you, so you need to continue trusting, just be careful."

"Become a better person and be sure to know who you are, before meeting someone new and hoping that person knows who you are."

"Don't struggle so much, best things happen when not expected."

"If I knew that today would be the last time I'd see you, I would hug you tight and pray the Lord be the keeper of your soul. If I knew that this would be the last time you pass through this door, I'd embrace you, kiss you, and call you back for one more. If I knew that this would be the last time I would hear your voice, I'd take hold of each word to be able to hear it over and over again. If I knew this is the last time I see you, I'd tell you I love you, and would not just assume foolishly you know it already."
— **Gabriel García Márquez**

It happens to the best of us, especially if you've been with the same person for a long time: either sex has tailed off completely or it's simply become a little stale. You know what works but you've become afraid of mixing it up and trying new things. But here, sexpert Tracey Cox, who has a range of products, gives her top tips for making your sex life feel exciting again.

13. <u>Keeping the relationship fresh</u>

1. Get away   Make a pact to go away for the weekend once every six weeks and you'll fix most of your sex and relationship problems. That was the stand-out advice of the most respected therapists in the US when asked to reveal the one thing they thought most helped save a struggling relationship. 80% percent said weekends away. It doesn't need to be expensive, just get you out of your usual environment where all the problems are (work, money, kids, stress). Make a pact with other couples to take turns and look after each other's kids and if a weekend is too ambitious, aim for one night, once a month in a decent hotel nearby.

2. Keep it fun   The more fun you have together, the more in love you will be. Once people decide they're serious about each other, they start getting serious about life: get a mortgage, have children. The relationship moves from 'fun' to 'functional': we stop concentrating on the relationship and concentrate on work and money.

Most couples skid into boring behaviour patterns around the two year mark - and it can be the kiss of death. When someone says "I don't know what happened but I've fallen out of love for no good reason", this is what's usually happened. Routine has killed the relationship. Get into the habit of planning at least two new activities to do together a month: theatre, a show, trying new restaurants, watching films.

3. Small gestures go a long way   It really is the little things that count. A recent study of more than 5,000 people found small gestures of love - like making a cup of tea - are more important than big, grand romantic displays for long-term love and happiness. Cooking her favourite meal when she's down, or planning a spa day when they've been working so hard - simple, thoughtful gestures mean a lot.

4. Do exciting things   Long-term love is a kind, soft, comfy emotion. Lust, on the other hand, is primitive, wild and edgy. We need risk and a hint of danger to continue to see our partners as sexual beings. The more shocking and liable to get the old heart thudding, the better - it is possible to shock your brain into falling back into lust. Any type of adrenalin boosting activity drives up the dopamine level in your brain, making you feel lustier and more in love. So do anything that slightly freaks you out – sky-dive, book a day driving on a race track, ride a pushbike through traffic, kick-box, play fight, jump on a roller coaster, even wearing your hot pink skyscraper wedges to the office.

5. No more excuses   Stop making excuses about being too busy - there is time for sex. Aim for 10 minutes a few times a week and one longer session (even 30 minutes works) once a fortnight. That's even less time than watching one hour-long TV show a week. Have 'bite sized' sex: It doesn't have to have a beginning, middle and end. Kissing counts too.

6. Act on a flicker of desire   You sort of wouldn't mind if you had sex? Don't just ponder the thought, pounce on it – and do it as soon as you can. Studies show the more time that passes between having an idea and following up on it, the more likely you are to lose motivation. I'm not saying you should burst into your partner's board meeting and drag him out by the tie, but don't let things like dishes or the meal being ready or 'I'll just answer that email first' get in the way.

When you go through a breakup, the first few hours, days, and weeks can be so overwhelming that it's hard to know what to do with yourself. There are some steps you can use to take care of yourself in the aftermath.

14. How To Survive A Break-up (Because You Will)

Understand that you're going to feel loss.

1. Keep yourself busy.

2. Reach out to others for support.

3. Do a digital detox – delete messages, photos, etc.

4. Change your physical space.

5. Don't have breakup sex with the Ex.

6. Plan something fun — without your Ex

7. Reflect on your relationship – once the immediate pain has passed.

15. <u>10 Ways to Help Children Look After Their Mental Health</u>

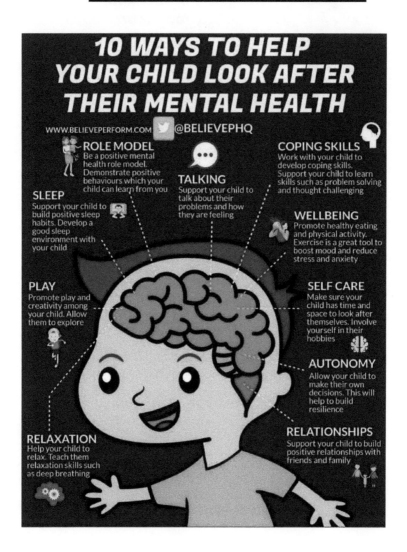

Fun for Seniors

16. <u>The secret to enjoying a long life:</u>

<u>12 steps to help you be happy in later life</u>

1. If you think of yourself as old, you will be old. The media will bang on about dementia and loneliness, but ignore them. Concentrate on the upside.

2. Take yourself out of your comfort zone. Resist being pigeonholed; keep experimenting; challenge yourself and society's stereotyping of you.

3. Try to stay healthy. Eat well and take lots of exercise – it's good for brain and body. Exercise doesn't have to mean playing competitive ice hockey; the odd brisk walk will keep you in shape.

4. Look for positive role models. Helen Mirren, David Attenborough and, best of all, Michelangelo, who lived until the ripe old age (in 16th-century terms) of 88 and spent the final 20 years of his life designing and overseeing the construction of St Peter's Basilica in Rome. Now that's a way to go out.

5. Seek to become the person you always wanted to be. One reason many people are at their happiest in their 60s is that they feel freer and less beholden to others. They contain all their previous selves and can start to make sense of them.

6. Don't just maintain social connections with your own age group: mix across the generations as much as you can. Inter-generational contact has become increasingly difficult, but if we can do it we benefit – and society benefits.

7. Be willing to let stuff go. If that friendship isn't working, drop it. Streamline your life. There is less time left, so make it count.

8. Ageing should be a process of opening rather than closing doors. "We will lose some things – speed, stamina, a bit of mental agility – but in many other respects we gain," says Honoré. We learn new skills, have greater social awareness, are likely to be more altruistic, are "lighter" in our approach to life – because we are less hung up on creating a good impression – and can see the bigger picture. It may be that we are in a position to make a greater contribution to society in our 60s and 70s than in our so-called prime.

9. Honesty is the best policy. Don't try to pretend you are not 75 or 85 or whatever age you are. "As soon as we start lying about our age, we're giving the number a terrible power – a power it doesn't deserve," says Honoré. People do it because there are so many ageist assumptions attached to age, but the way to fight back is to subvert those assumptions.

10. Society tells us that love and romance belong to the young, but it's not true. …and plenty of older people continue to experience the joy of sex. But there are no rules: have as much – or as little – as you want. Some older people see it as a blessed release to escape the shackles of falling in love (and lust), but others can't imagine life without it. Whatever turns you on.

11. Ignore people who say you can't teach an old dog new tricks. You can. Despite the common perception that creativity is the preserve of the young, we can get more creative as we get older. Our neural networks loosen up and we have the confidence and freedom to challenge groupthink. Honoré was encouraged last year when the Turner prize abolished its age limit for artists. Michelangelo could have been a contender.

12. Don't pretend death isn't coming. Embrace it – just not yet. "It's useful to know our lives are bookended," says Honoré. "When time is running out, it becomes more precious. It gives life shape and, in some ways, meaning." Don't dwell morbidly on it, but don't shy away from it either. The closer you get to it, the less you are likely to fear it and the greater your focus will be on the things that really matter.

About the Author

Harj Mahil is a normal British man who has enjoyed 35 years in the business world.

After graduating, he gained ten years of invaluable experience in Tesco's commercial team ("Buying Controller" during the time they overtook Sainsbury as the UK's leading food retailer by market share), and finished his corporate career with ten years helping the NHS to reduce product costs. In between were spells with BP, Booker and RHM, alongside some time as a Business Advisor to the Prince's Trust.

Harj also set-up and ran a café/catering business, which gave him further experience and opportunities to test and develop his tips for survival and success.

In 2016, he set up a Serviced Accommodation business (SA), and then when the Covid-19 pandemic struck, he managed to transform the business into a more sustainable one, better able to withstand uncertain times and recessions.

Whilst it's been a tough time for many, opportunities now exist to create better days. Harj feels that the tips in this book, to which he himself continuously refers, could help others also realise their hopes and dreams, and achieve the life they want.

The tips featured here are literally those that have helped see and guide him through the hard times, and inspired and motivated when times are good. When he has shared them with others - the response has been extremely encouraging.

With this in mind he wants to share his tips more widely, to give anyone looking for guidance in a **quick reference format**, something easy to navigate and understand without having to bury their heads in large manuals and detailed study. That they can do if they want to find more detail.

Harj's enthusiasm and thirst for knowledge has enabled him to pick up practical tips from many successful people and mentors. They have helped him to achieve his dreams.

There is no reason why they can't help do the same for you!

Lightning Source UK Ltd.
Milton Keynes UK
UKHW050211191122
412430UK00007B/151/J